THE PORTAGE POETRY
SERIES

Series Titles

Mourning
Dokubo Melford Goodhead

Messengers of the Gods: New and Selected Poems
Kathryn Gahl

After the 8-Ball
Colleen Alles

Careful Cartography
Devon Bohm

Broken On the Wheel
Barbara Costas-Biggs

Sparks and Disperses
Cathleen Cohen

Holding My Selves Together: New and Selected Poems
Margaret Rozga

Lost and Found Departments
Heather Dubrow

Marginal Notes
Alfonso Brezmes

The Almost-Children
Cassondra Windwalker

Meditations of a Beast
Kristine Ong Muslim

Praise for
Dokubo Melford Goodhead

Whether it is his native country of Nigeria or the home he has made in America, Dokubo Goodhead's *Mourning* is an unflinching examination of loss, grief, and yearning for ancestral roots. From a famed icon like Kobe Bryant to the epistolary poem to his little sister, Dokubo transcends the human heart through what is universal to all of us: a reflection of our mortality and bearing witness to those we have lost. *Mourning* is a magnificent body of work which angers yet soothes us in our times of need.

—Genaro Kỳ Lý Smith
author of *The Land Baron's Sun: The Story of Lý Loc and His Seven Wives*, and *The Land South of the Clouds*

This is a collection of powerful poems about loss and grief. "& despair was everywhere/followed me everywhere/like my own skin." Goodhead's poems are devastating and striking. And, so, so beautiful.

—Chika Unigwe
author of *On Black Sisters Street*

In these times of upheaval and tragedy, Dokubo Goodhead's work fulfills that most basic, ancient need of poetry: it gives voice to our collective grief and our resistance to injustice. These modern odes speak to the heroes of our day in the face of wrong. It's work that understands its place in timeless epic cycles while being rooted in our current day. It is what we need most now.

—Doug Schnitzspahn
Editor-in-Chief, *Elevation Outdoors Magazine*

Poet of the past, poet of the waters, poet of the familiar and the unfamiliar, massacres, famine, family and friends, in Goodhead's powerfully lyrical poetry, we come to grips with language that vividly conveys the sense of loss, grief, pain, and anguish. The poet reaches to the very depths of his emotions to reach a place of renewal and redemption.

—Uduma Kalu
poet, critic, and journalist
former literary editor of *The Guardian*, Lagos

MOURNING

Poems by
Dokubo Melford Goodhead

Cornerstone Press
Stevens Point, Wisconsin

Cornerstone Press, Stevens Point, Wisconsin 54481
Copyright © 2022 Dokubo Melford Goodhead
www.uwsp.edu/cornerstone

Printed in the United States of America by
Point Print and Design Studio, Stevens Point, Wisconsin 54481

Library of Congress Control Number: 2022933512
ISBN: 978-1-7377390-9-8

All rights reserved.

An earlier version of "Letter to My Little Sister" was first published in *Nigeria World* (Friday, November 11, 2005): https://nigeriaworld.com/articles/2005/nov/110.html

Cornerstone Press titles are produced in courses and internships offered by the Department of English at the University of Wisconsin–Stevens Point.

DIRECTOR & PUBLISHER EXECUTIVE EDITOR
Dr. Ross K. Tangedal   Jeff Snowbarger

SENIOR EDITORS
Lexie Neeley, Monica Swinick, Kala Buttke

SENIOR PRESS ASSISTANT
Gavrielle McClung

PRESS STAFF
Rhiley Block, Alyssa Bronk, Grace Dahl, Patrick Fogarty, Ava Freeman, Angela Green, Brett Hill, Cale Jacoby, Hunter Keisow, Adam King, Jeremy Kremser, Amanda Leibham, Leo McEvilly, Abbi Rohde, Abbi Wasielewski, Bethany Webb

To
Bekinwari, my mother
Mysister, my grandmother
the late Mr. Justice M.D. Goodhead, my father

the poorest of the poor of the oil archipelago
of islands of the Niger Delta
& their counterparts in the rest of the Niger Delta

the polluted & dead rivers
of the Niger Delta & Ken Saro-Wiwa, who paid the ultimate
price for his courage.

Contents

In America
The Comet Goes into Orbit 2
I am George Floyd 3
Ode to a Warrior 4
Sacrifice 6

The Return of the Past
The Road Home 10

Notes on the Post-Colonial Homeland
Elegy for M.C. 18
Ode to a Brother 20
Death and the Raft Man 22
Whistle on the Savannah 24
The Wailing Woman 27
Wraiths 28
The Lekki Massacre 30
A Song of Sorrow for Maxwell Oditta 31
Mourning Kimse 42
Letter to My Little Sister 44
What Year? 93
Confused 94
You Died 95
The Fallen City 96
Forgive Me, Mother 97
Looking for the Hiding Place of Death 98
I Never Saw the Fisher of Sorrows 99
The Road Before Me 100
No Longer a Boy 101
In Memoriam – for Mother 102
The Man Who Came From Death to Life 104

Notes 107
Acknowledgments 119

In America

The Comet Goes into Orbit

For Kobe Bryant

Candlelight leaping in the wind.
Standing on the threshold, a prodigy.
A basketball in one arm; the other arm akimbo.
Toiling and toiling and toiling until
The last drop of sweat is spent
For the soaring flights and feats of genius
That leave the jaw hanging in the air.
Such was the coming of the comet.
Light from a million cell phones
Light up the scene, the mourning paths, the arena.
So brief the candlelight
But the comet has gone into orbit.

I am George Floyd

For George Floyd

From the spearpoint of your knee against my carotid artery,
I cry out to you, am I not a man like you? Am I not a man like you?
You have planted a mountain on the passageway of my life blood
and my spirit cries out on the threshold of departure,
Am I not a man? Am I not a man?

Darkness is fast descending here on the threshold of your naked terror
and my body struggles for life like an animal in a death trap.
O author of this senseless terror, am I not a man like you?
Am I not a man like you?

My voice cries out like the voice of the one crying in the wilderness,
Am I not a man? O God of mercy, am I not a man?
Is there not a soul out there to lift this mountain off my neck?
O God of mercy, is there not a brother or a sister
out there to lift this mountain off my neck?
Is there not a soul in this world to cry with me,
set me free from the cold hands of the descending darkness?
   Lift this mountain off my neck.

I can't breathe. I can't breathe. I can't breathe.
My brain is descending into turbulent darkness.
Life is slipping away here on concrete and asphalt,
the knee of my executioner heavy upon my neck
like a mountain, a crushing prison from which escape is impossible.

Night is coming. Night is coming.
And like a trapped animal waiting for the end,
I find that I cannot struggle anymore.
But just before night falls, I summon the last of my departing breath
from my violated body, make my final cry.

O racists of the earth, O racists of the earth!
O you who would smite a man to death
for nothing other than the color of his skin,
Am I not a man? Am I not a man?

Ode to a Warrior

For Chadwick Boseman

Brother, I heard the news of your death yesterday—
sudden waves crashing upon the shore
on an otherwise uneventful day,
an overcast sky happening suddenly on a bright day.
Shock, bewilderment, a tempest batters the lighthouse.
Brother, you were a mountaineer still scaling the mountain
        of your youth,
reaching for new heights as mountaineers do, old peaks
forgotten, the new peak the tale of the day.
For many of us, brother, the old peaks
you had left behind we would take with absolute *joie de vivre*,
crying, "What now? What else is there to be done
on this side of Heaven's gates?"
But for you, King T'Challa, King of Wakanda, there were
still many mountaintops to conquer, many peaks
on this side of Heaven's gates.
Up and up and up, ranger of the towering peaks,
you made your way.
O brother, who sought to keep company with the eagle,
King of the sky!
You set your eyes upon new peaks
and you climbed, taking nothing with you
but the spirit of the great warrior.
That is why, brother, sorrow sits with its twin at the fireplace,
where storytellers duel one another
to tell stories of your life, lived too in the trenches
where courage meets the killer.
Four long years, brother.
Four long years, brother.
You battled the killer
and would not give up your assegai
or your shield.

Mourning

You held the treacherous pass, you held the sacred ground,
you held the passage between life
and death. You gave no foothold
to the killer.
Now, brother, the horn of the warrior goes before you,
messenger
running ahead of you to Heaven's gates. O brother! O brother!
Wakanda forever!

Sacrifice
For Health Workers Who Died Fighting COVID-19

The year was a year of death.
The virus moved through the land
cutting a wide swath of death
wherever it set up camp. A mask
was shown to work like a shield
against it but many would not wear it,
even for love of their neighbors,
even for the thought that they could
succumb to the fire of the virus.

'No one can tell me what to do,'
they said. 'I will not be a victim
of government overreach.' & so,
the virus raged through the land,
filling the hospitals with the sick
& the dying. Many died, leaving
too soon for those they loved.

Amongst the dead were many
brave men & women, who
stood in the line of fire.
& fought day and night
   to keep the grim reaper
from overrunning the line of fire,
breaking the dam, flooding
  the community with the sick
to make every home & every street
in the land a place of mourning.

These brave men & women
put their shoulders to the burden.

Mourning

  & held the line of fire.
  & held the line of fire.
Many fell in the line of fire
before the shout of victory
over the battlefield, over the battlefield.

Sister, the brave have fallen on the battlefield—
heroes in the war against
 a mighty plague.
May a grateful nation pause
for a moment each year
   to remember their sacrifice,

that generations of their countrymen
& women coming after them
may see in them the example
of ultimate sacrifice.

The Return of the Past

The Road Home

For Ben Watkins

I approach the other side of this aging body,
denied of the things that I most wanted to do when I was about your age
the day I discovered in the school choir that I had suffered
a sudden metamorphosis—
my voice had gone from treble

to bass
overnight.

Kyrie eleison, kyrie eleison, kyrie eleison.

A wife, my buddy and best friend, and a couple of other buddies,
my children. But the hand of misfortune was heavy upon me, setting me
up for tragedy:

a walk alone to Golgotha—
a three-year battle with the nation's exam body, during which my grade
in Biology went from A2 to C5 to F9. I thought, young brother,
that I was in a fantastic world but the hounds of misfortune
showed me no smiling face.

Three years on the road to Golgotha:
a walk alone in the severest trial of my young life—
my health was taken from me.

The angel of despair raised his horn,
blew it as loud as he could in my ear,
and on my path.

& despair was everywhere,
followed me everywhere
like my own skin,
wrestled me in the night and in the day laid ambush for me.

Mourning

You are going nowhere,
said the angel of death. Kyrie eleison. Kyrie eleison.
Kyrie eleison.

Three years on the treacherous road
before the West African Examination Council
said to me: "We are sorry, young man. It was a typographical error."

Mr. Esezobor, Mrs. Lufadeju, guardian angels at the last barricade,
when my life hung by a thread, they rescued me
from that house of torture,
the house of lies and everything corrupt, of come tomorrow,
and come next week.
& I lived. But my health was shattered.
Three years of living with the horror

of horrors

& the treasure trove
was gone.

Stomach ulcer. Heartburns that shook up my body like
angina pectoris. Malaria that came knocking on the door every other week,
with constant dozing off that not even the wonder drug of the day,

Fansidar,

could beguile away. I felt like Job in the hour of his trial.

Kyrie eleison. Kyrie eleison. Kyrie eleison.

But the worst was yet to come. The road to Golgotha is a cruel road.
A bad decision about when to take my exams,
& I lost the company of Hippocrates and with that the dream to become
the doctor of the beleaguered islands of the oil archipelago,

going from island to island to treat the sick,
a faithful German shepherd, Wolf, by my side.

Dokubo Melford Goodhead

The road to Golgotha is a cruel road.

Kyrie eleison. Kyrie eleison. Kyrie eleison.

From Golgotha,
I picked up myself
and put my feet on the road to Emmaus.

I returned to the lions' den, back in the land of the rolling hills
There, where lions roam, the hyenas roam too.
There I was brought to Golgotha itself.
The vandals of the sea rolled like an evil wave
into my hostel room.

Flat on my belly, they had me on the ground,
the executioner's pistol pointing at my head.
They say that at the last hour of a man, his world flashes before
his eyes like a dream or one long montage.
Such a man must be in a peaceful place,
the end slipping into the homestead like the gentle sea breezes
that steal one away into an afternoon sleep.

When sudden death accosts you, there is no such montage
Everything freezes. The world stands still. The second lasts forever
The waves wash upon you but you do not hear the cry of the seabirds

or the call of the ancient boatman.
The world is a frozen glass.

Five young men, travelers on the road that leads nowhere,
one with a ceremonial sword, one with a machete,
one with a broken water pipe. & then there
was the executioner, with his pistol,
and the Capo, who stood somewhere there,
solemn like Al Capone, surveying everything.
They held me hostage, took everything from me
that I called a possession,

Mourning

save a shirt, a pair of pants, and a file jacket.

But just before the clock ticked down
 to the final second,
the lone gunshot to the head
& the moment of departure from the darkening plain,
the Capo became a peacemaker.
Let him live, he said. What we came for,
we've got. To kill an innocent man
when you have robbed him of everything is to put an albatross
around your neck.

Remember, my friends, the "Rime of the Ancient Mariner."
'It is an ancient Mariner,
And he stoppeth one of three.
'By the long grey beard and glittering eye…'
And, so, I lived to tell my tale,
while the vandals of the sea sailed

into the night.

The company of Hippocrates gone,
all my worldly goods gone,
I was once more a raft man
cast adrift on the turbulent sea,

but the Capo
turned priest
turned poet

had given me life.
Remember the "Rime of the Ancient Mariner."
So, I put my feet on the road to life,
left Golgotha behind me. Kyrie eleison. Kyrie eleison.

The years passed and life gave me all the good things a young man
could ask for—a job after one's heart, cars, a place of one's
own and what the French call *joie de vivre*.

Dokubo Melford Goodhead

There it was—the American Dream.

I was far away from Golgotha,
or so I thought. The suffering of Job was behind me,
or so I thought. But, soon, the drums of the place
of suffering were beating again for me.

The road of Golgotha is a cruel road.
O Brother, O Sister, the road of Golgotha is a cruel road.
The storms of Golgotha battered me again.
They baptized me in wave upon wave of terror
& blinding darkness.

O fortune, O (mis)fortune, your hand has been heavy upon me.

The lightning came.
Gave me a hard slap in the face.
The thunder came,
almost blew out my eardrums
with a well-timed blow.

The storms of Golgotha
swept away everything – the place of my own
in the poshest part of the city.
Some call it the crown jewel of the city,
cars, savings, rainy-day funds, my life's savings,
health, even the joy of living.

But I have known kindness too
on this dark and stormy road home,
from Barbados and Tema and Accra
 and Lomé and Northampton to the shores of this great country.

Kyrie eleison. Kyrie eleison. Kyrie eleison.

I have known the gift of brotherhood.
I have known the gift of friendship.

Mourning

I have known the persistent phone call asking, O Brother, where are you?
& O Brother, how are you?

I remember his voice. I knew his voice. I knew when he would be calling.
I knew that he would call until I pick up the phone.

There are those who stand at the gates of sorrow,
rent their garments and weep with one,
take on the yoke of suffering with one.
O Brother, where are you?

Kyrie eleison. Kyrie eleison. Kyrie eleison.

Oh, Ben Watkins, you died. Orphan.
My hero. Only fourteen years old.
Tragedy had taken your mother and father away from

you in the cruelest manner.
Golgotha came to you and you bore
its blows on your young chest.
Survived the calamity to tell your tale
of life, of joy, of a chef's dream.

Then came the vagabond killer
Angiomatoid fibrous histiocytoma.
You were one of only six on earth
with the disease. 7.8 billion people

on earth

& you were one of only six
with the vagabond killer.
Golgotha came, Golgotha came, Golgotha came
& you fought but the vagabond killer
took you away.

Dokubo Melford Goodhead

Young warrior, young brother, Ben Watkins, I read your story
& felt the surge of the sea.
The warrior fights to the end.
The warrior thrusts out his chest
and takes the blows of life
like storm-battered seabirds
take the battering of sea storms,
spread out their wings and fly.

The road to Emmaus is a long distance away.
The road home is a long distance away.
Spread before the traveler on the road of Golgotha
is the valley of sorrows, the mountain ranges of despair,
& the clop, clop, drip, drip, of the well-worn shoes

of the traveler

& his rain-soaked garments.

Young warrior, young brother, Ben Watkins, I read your story
& felt the surge of the sea.
Kyrie eleison. Kyrie eleison. Kyrie eleison.

Notes on the
Post-Colonial Homeland

Elegy for M.C.

I hear the school bell ringing
   in the school down
in the valley where school
   children nurse dreams
as high as the peaks of Mt. Kilimanjaro.
   I see the school children
marching at a solemn pace,
   their heads tucked
into their chests at half-mast.

On eight youthful shoulders
   the gleaming mahogany casket sits.
A light rain. The sun. The pallbearers march
   in a straight line to the stirring beat
of the ode to John Brown.

A light rain is falling. The earth
   is a bit sodden. & not a cheek
is dry, as the pallbearers take
   the great man through the familiar
places where he raised a generation
   of men and women.

A 'twin brother' of the great
   Winston, he rallied his boys and girls
to the mark again and again.

Child, pick up yourself
   from defeat! Up! Join the fray.
Idle moments are for the dead.

We measure longevity
   not by how long we have lived,
but by the miles of goodness
   we have done in the lives of others.

Mourning

These words used to resound
   in the confines of a plain
high-school assembly hall.
   Now the voice that uttered
them has fallen silent and he who uttered them
   now belongs to the ages.

I turn away from the mourning
   of the schoolchildren and wipe a tear
from my face. I put both hands
   to my face, a praying mantis
in a posture of prayer,
   and weep and weep until
the clouds pass and the sun
   peeks through the dancing leaves.

He was a Nwalimu—
   a teacher of teachers;
the best of his generation.
   Now, he embarks on the great march
to eternity and his words
   & deeds belong to the Ages.

Ode to a Brother

For Sam Iroanusi

I have been diminished
  by your passing,
O Brother, &
my heart is splitting
thunderbolts like
the ax of a woodsman
falling upon stubborn wood.

The weather is foul.
The hurricane is so hard upon the rocks,
the vengeful rain is splitting rocks
as ancient as the first rivers.
The seagulls are frantically
beating their wings
against the raging of the hurricane.
Their cries can be heard all the way
to the ends of the earth.

I wish I had not been cast
upon this deserted island, O Brother,
where seaside rocks roar
as loudly as the raging sea.

But, then, what could I do
against decades of noxious fumes
from the mad thing upon the porch?[1]
You had to use it to live
and it turned your lungs
  into broken sieves,
a fisherman's tattered nets
hung upon a scarecrow.

O Brother. In-law/Brother.
Several times I have dreamt of the passing of the plague,
of this great trial that robbed me

Mourning

of job, of home, of being in the world,
and you and I shooting the breeze
   at a house by the sea,
watching the waves come to shore
  like horses dragging their chariots
     to the finish line.

Sunsets over the tranquil sea.
Golden waves taking the seafarer
home to hearths where the bread
of love is broken.

But now, what can I do,
    O Brother?
Alone on this treacherous island,
I mourn your passing like
beleaguered seagulls frantically
     beating their wings
against a raging storm.

The sea is rushing to shore.
  Treacherous waves
 overwhelm the house by the sea.
I will hear your gentle voice
     again & cry,
O God of mercy, let the thunder break,
let the lightning break, let the raging water break,
  upon the troubled shore.

Let me weep for you,
O Brother, until the raging river
returns to the sea.
O Brother, let me weep for you,
until the raging river
  returns to the sea
    & my heart beating
 its wings like seagulls
riding the terror of the storm
return to the hearth by the tranquil sea.

Death and the Raft Man

Through the fog
on a stormy day at sea,
a raft man, his raft wrecked by a violent storm,
was drifting to a savage end,
when, suddenly, he saw a light.

Desperately, the beleaguered man tried to steer the mangled raft
toward the light. In this impossible task,
good fortune for once lent a hand
to the dying man and the raft
   drifted toward the light.

Getting close to the light,
  the raft man cried
into the stormy night,
Mayday, Mayday, Mayday.

The words were still on the lips
  of the raft man when the light
vanished into the stormy night.
  Thunder take you to your watery grave!,
the raft man heard voices say
from where the light had been.

The fever was upon the raft man
and forth and back he went from the land of the dead.
Just before he slipped across the shadowy plain again,
the raft man
lifted his voice and cried into the foul night,
nothing but the wind, nothing but the sea, nothing but the darkness,
  nothing but the phantoms of dead sea men.

The words were still on the lips
   of the raft man,
when a strange and terrible voice cried into the tempestuous night,

Mourning

the first day of May is the day of the dead.
  The first day of May is the day of the dead.

The sea roared again, baring its fangs
  to the forbidding night.
Delirious, hardly conscious, the dying man
  cried again, Mayday, Mayday, Mayday.

Whistle on the Savannah

For McPhilip Nwachukwu

The news came today
that he had started the long walk
   across the gray
Savannah & my spirit
sank. Sisyphus' stone, rolling down the hill
into the great depths
   of the timeless river.

He was my friend,
a gentle soul that loved
the life of the mind. He loved
the consolation of the
   'fireside'
intellectual moments.

We thought of the
   great tradition & wondered whether
we could ever produce
anything of worth to continue
the great tradition of the mind and the house of
literature;
so that just like the stars of those
who went before us now shine
 so brightly & lift our spirits
   to strive for the higher mark,
we too would, striving, leave
   some mark no matter
how modest that they who are coming after us
   may not say that we
   are a misbegotten generation.

Now he is gone on the lone
ranger's journey across the graying earth,
   and I struck numb

Mourning

as if by a sudden clap of thunder
look for ways to make sense
   of his passing.

But as I took the quiet walk,
my head thrust into my breast,
I thought I heard his footsteps
  behind me & the familiar voice say,
   O Brother, keep up
the good fight, knowing that each of us

  has but a brief moment on this Savannah
& then are gone.

Leave those needless fights
    that task the mind & soul
but add nothing to the man
  or to the commonwealth
  to others.

Walk by them. & if you can,
run, so that by salvaging the time,
  dear friend, you may take
  what little amount of provision
  that has been made out to you
from the store of the ancient time
  keeper & making it count,
  live every day a free man.

That, O Brother, is our charge,
 so that when the great whistle
  sounds across this vast Savannah,
you may, leaving it all, walk
   with your head unbowed,
    knowing that you have fought
the good fight and fought
     it well.

Dokubo Melford Goodhead

& in the hour,
  in the hour
 of passing, Cry, O God,
may my path lead from the vast Savannah
to the mighty shores
  of Heaven's gates,
my work done,
  my spirit light with the consolation
   of a time well spent
    on this timeless Savannah.

The Wailing Woman

*For the Woman Wailing
at the Polling Booth*

I hear the cry of the disconsolate woman,
breaking the day, breaking the tense noon.
What country this that turns elections
into occasions for the dirge maker?
I hear the woman crying. I hear the woman crying.
It strikes me and opens up a cavern
~~deep~~ inside me, where the town crier
wails and mourns with the woman
crying in the middle of the day.

Wraiths[2]

I heard the weaverbird sing this morning,
in the moment between the land of sleep
and waking to the call of the morning.
I heard the weaverbird sing. I heard the weaverbird sing its
ancient song,
        its ancient song,
        its ancient song.
       The same song
   that it sang when I was a little boy,
     when I was a little boy
growing up on a little island, ancient and peaceful,
  then, in the oil archipelago of the Niger Delta.
  'The world is so difficult, the world is so difficult,'
the weaverbird sang, the weaverbird sang. I knew the song by heart
   from my years as a little boy on a little island
   listening to the ancient bird
sing its ancient song, its ancient song, its ancient song;
so, I sang along with it. I sang the ancient song.
& immediately I was a child once more, running through
the arteries of an ancient island in a laughing archipelago,
in a laughing archipelago, in a laughing archipelago,
     chasing the weaverbird
   from footpath to footpath.
      O ancient bird, little friend of my childhood,
     sent to comfort me in the hour of trial,
    O weaverbird, O weaverbird,
      I hear your song.
      I hear your song.
      I hear your song
in a basement on the corner of Fifteenth Avenue

Mourning

in the emerald city. In the emerald city.
    O ancient bird, O ancient bird, O ancient bird from
    a now lost era of an archipelago, where now sea
winds cry like ancient wraiths over blood-soaked islands,
    over the slain, over shuttered schools, over ghost playgrounds:
'The oil wells have gobbled up everything.
    The broken oil pipelines
have given birth to a wasteland. The seabirds are gone.
The fish are gone. The people are gone
 to the slums of haunted cities.
    & now only the hermit crab remains,
     only the hermit crab remains
   running here & running there
    on blood-soaked sands on deserted shores
    in the oil archipelago.'

The Lekki Massacre[3]

The steel boots came like thieves
in the middle of the night
and set the god of war upon the roses.
Terror unfolded its maws and went to work.
In the dark hour. In the dark hour.
The asphalt road became a river.
The river became a wailing tree
with the blood of the fallen,
with the blood of the roses.
Dead men they say tell no tales
but the blood of the children
of the black October will continue
to wail in the town square
until morning comes to a sick country.

A Song of Sorrow for Maxwell Oditta[4]

I heard of your death the
   other day
and was shocked to my marrows
      as if a clap of thunder
  had given me a slap
that rang in my ears for eternity.

So, I heard of the death of
     our great friend, McPhilip,
  and on that day,
like today, wandered through a maze
    of pathways with none of them
      leading anywhere.

I feel like a stranded whale
  at a waterside.
The sea stands before me
  but all I feel is the agony of loss.

I am suffering from grief that stinks
    like a urine-soaked garment
      on the back of a wayfarer
that has just seen one of those creatures
  with a thousand heads
  & a thousand mouths
that suddenly springs out of nowhere
     to waylay the traveler
    going down the lonely path.

O the treacherous misfortunes
      that lay
    sudden ambush
   to the spirit!
So is the news of your death to me,
   my dear friend,
     Maxwell Oditta.

Dokubo Melford Goodhead

I call you by your name
that your spirit that still lingers
  on the threshold of departure
   may hear me & take solace
      for the journey before you.

What does the traveler
  traveling by himself down
    a forest path say when he is suddenly surprised
    by a creature with a thousand heads
    & a thousand mouths?

If he is unable to say a word because
  of the sudden shock
    of the marvelous sight,
  he is sure to return again to the place
  of the marvelous encounter.

So is the news of the sudden death
  of a dear friend,
   O Maxwell Oditta,
   my dear friend.

The mourning news
  does not let you be
  until you have poured out
all your grief and are
  left like a whale
  stranded at the waterside
  & all that is before you
     is nothing

   but the gray and restless sea.

  So, we bear the burden of grief.
     So, we bear the burden
of silence through a thousand moons,
through a thousand seasons
    for a dear one that we lose
       so suddenly.

Mourning

The fishermen
   will return
from their voyage
     to the great sea
& they will find me
still weeping by the sea.

Ah, my dear friend,
  may my words reach you
before your spirit departs
    on the journey before you.

Oh, my friend. Oh, my friend.
  These are not happy times
    in the oil archipelago.
Once more, brother,
  there are guns and gunboats
  in the oil archipelago.

Fighter jets are waiting
 to take to the skies,
    hawks of death, messengers of death,
    carriers of death,
   they are the gifts for the black gold
to us, creek dwellers, island dwellers,
     swamp dwellers,
    afterthought in the country
    that Lugard made.

We are the microminorities
   of the earth
     caught up in a world
created by others for themselves.

You see why my grief
  is a thousandfold, my friend.
News of your death is coming at a time
    when the drumbeats of genocide
       are once more exploding like thunderbolts
    in the oil archipelago.

Dokubo Melford Goodhead

The oil that has pauperized
  the fisherman &
famished the mothers,
  who used to leave before the cock crows, in the belly
      of the night,

to harvest periwinkles & oysters
    from bountiful creeks;
      but the oil must continue to flow
   even as we, children of the sea,
      children of the river,
  children of the waterside,
    become children of the
apocalyptic world that they have
made of once singing islands,
    where the laughter
        of children used to ring
    out in the creeks: now an archipelago of dead rivers
& killing islands.

Children
    of joy, full of joy, now casualties of the coming
        of the oil men.

O my dear friend, I grieve for you,
    I mourn
your sudden dying,
  I mourn
  the death of countless
      souls.

Victims of the terrors
  of the apocalypse, sacrifices
  to the oil god, who has decreed
    that the more the human sacrifices
      the sweeter the crude.

So, my friend, O my friend,
  the oil flows from rivers
inundated with death and from islands

Mourning

of a once happy archipelago,
 whose children now
disappear into the slums
    of jungle cities,
   where no one mourns them
      when they die.

Slums, where the dead,
heavy with the great burden
of not being mourned
stay for a thousand seasons
on the threshold of departure,
asking why it is that while
the invaders enjoy the wealth
of the black gold, the sweet crude,
  they are condemned to the
  apocalypse of its making.

 So, as I mourn you, my dear friend,
O Maxwell, O Maxwell, I mourn
too all those souls, disconsolate souls,
 on the thresholds of departure, bearers
 of an inconsolable grief, whose tears
 wash the mourning grounds.

I see them, nameless souls,
burdened with the grief of their great suffering,
while they wait
on the threshold
  of departure,
weeping, weeping on the mourning grounds,
    seeking reprieve
 from their crushing burden.

I see them, my dear friend,
    I see them.
& burdened with their grief,
grief that seizes the soul
and will not let go, I cry aloud,
'O Great One, give them

reprieve, for they have suffered
   too much in this world,
lived with death from the day
they were born until the day
      of their departure.'

They departed
from a world of the apocalypse,
where oil fires burn all day

and ancient pipelines spew death into the rivers,
turning everything into
a wasteland of death.
They headed for the slums,
from the oil archipelago,
where no one knows their names.

They died in wretched shacks,
where no one knew their names,
O my friend, O Maxwell. The moment of departure
from the darkling plain
came upon their doorsteps
& all they had was their poverty and their pain,
which they gathered about them
like a beggar gathers his rags about him
to make the journey
   out of the Apocalypse.

Ah, Maxwell, my friend,
do you know that the lives of the inhabitants of the once
   happy archipelago of islands
are now counted in oil wells and oil pipelines
   and oil barrels.

Bearers of man-made yokes,
they live by the light of hurricane lamps,
orphaned from electricity-bearing
   national power lines,
while those who do not live
in the shadow of the Apocalypse

Mourning

live by the light of national power lines,
set up with money drawn
    from the pipelines
        traversing
    their apocalyptic world.

Ah, my dear friend.
  Ah, Maxwell Oditta.
I mourn you. I mourn you. I mourn
      you.
  & I mourn
those who live
    in the shadow of death!

Ah, Maxwell, I mourn
your sudden death.
 I mourn your sudden departure.
I mourn your death like
one carrying a burden heavy
as the great humpback whale.

 I grieve for you, my friend.
   I grieve for you;
for now, I know that we
will not sit by the fireside
at the communal place at the waterside
  to tell stories of our lives
like one peels back the skins
of an onion skin by skin;
but never mind, my friend,
    the waterside
is now drenched with the black gold
   & the fish are all gone.

The crabs that once
raced back and forth
  on the sands of the waterside
are gone too,
carrying their homes
with them like refugees

carrying their bundles,
 the entirety of their worldly goods
 for the long journey before them.

Ah, Maxwell. O Maxwell,
even, my friend, the hermit crab,
has carried its burden and made
off to the great sea.
The river is not like it used to be,
it told me when it was departing
    with all of its family,
      like the inhabitants of a besieged city
         fleeing the city
  before it falls to the enemy.

O Maxwell. O Maxwell, my friend.
The hermit crab is gone.
 The hermit crab is gone.
 The hermit crab has left the oil archipelago
  with its entire family.

Ah, Maxwell. O Maxwell, my friend,
the hermit crab is gone.
& now all that is left for me
 is the world of the Apocalypse.

Ah, Maxwell. O Maxwell.
How long ago is it now
that we came from the soothing ocean
of our mothers' wombs
into a world of green forests
  & laughing islands?

Now, those who despise us
have turned our world
into a world of Apocalypse now
and Apocalypse ever after?

O Maxwell. O Maxwell, my friend.
I no longer marvel

Mourning

at the capacity of man
to inflict misery and death
on his fellow men.

O Maxwell. O Maxwell, my friend.
Even if I live for ten thousand seasons,
I will not marvel anymore.
I carry a burden. I carry a burden
that keeps me awake all night & into the early
hours of the morning,
when the cocks crow
& usher in another day of sorrow.

O Maxwell. O Maxwell, my friend.
My friend the hermit crab is gone!
O Maxwell. O Maxwell, my friend.
My friend the hermit crab is gone!

So, I sing of grief.
I sing of my grief.
I sing of those dying in the Apocalypse.
I sing for the future.
I sing for those not yet born.
Will they come into such a cruel world
& live with such misery,
with such pain?

O thunder, give me voice!
O seven-headed hurricane, give me voice!
O mighty winds from the great sea,
give me voice to sing for those
who live in the shadow of death.
O grief, give me voice
to sing for those who live
in the world of the Apocalypse.

Once there was a boy,
 who ran about free in those creeks
that now reek of sorrow
& death. The laughter of the boy

used to ring out in those creeks,
boisterous laughter that made
the seabirds sing & the
laughter of other boys
to ring throughout the creeks.

So, it used to be, my departing friend.
So, it used to be, my departing friend,
where now people live in the shadow of death
& of the man-made Apocalypse.
Of sweet crude, of death crude.

The parrot that used to live
  in the coconut tree is gone.
The weaverbird that used to sing
  in the homestead all day long is gone.
The island robins that swarmed
the island skies are gone.
The seagulls that made mating calls
all day long are gone.
The herons that dove into the water
after the fish are gone.
All that is left of the oil archipelago
  is the sorrow & stench
of death on the river,
 death in the creeks,
 & death on the sea.

But the oil must flow
    in pipelines
that carry them
    to cities of light
on the breaking backs of islands
    that live in darkness.

The oil archipelago & its islands
see nothing but the bright lights
of the oil platforms.
The oil archipelago & its islands
   see nothing

Mourning

but the ghoulish lights
  of gas-flaring pipes.
The night comes, carrying
with it the ghostly lights
    of hurricane lamps and torchlights.

Ah, Maxwell. O Maxwell,
go in peace. Travel well,
    my friend,
   while I turn the grief
    that I feel for you
    into a dirge
      to sing for those
who live in the
  shadow of death,
in the shadow
    of the man-made
        Apocalypse.

Mourning Kimse

For Kimse Okoko

The eagle has departed from the homestead.
The sure-handed voyager has set his raft on the great sea.
The sea birds are calling to one another in the oil archipelago
and on the footpaths leading to the homestead,
and at the gate leading into the homestead,
and at the great courtyard, men, women, and children
weep for the great raft man of the oil archipelago.
Kimse! Kimse! Kimse!

The elders beat their bosoms with bare palms.
  Their tears fall to the earth
like heavy drops of rain from an overcast sky.
Raft man, who stood guard over the mouth of the river,
O lion of the oil archipelago,
you held the staff on behalf of a beleaguered people,
island people of the oil archipelago,
where dead rivers weep
and sea birds mourn the great dying
of an archipelago,
where laughter once stretched from creek to creek
into the horizon.
Kimse! Kimse! Kimse!

Seafarers, canoe people, raft people,
guardians of the sea—stood tall before
earth and sky
before the jackboots of colonialism set the trampling tide
on the archipelago,
bringing the flare of gas in the day, the flare of gas in the night,
oil spills by day, oil spills by night, oil spills on the morning tide,
& broken pipes
that spew black death on the mourning tide.
Kimse! Kimse! Kimse!

Mourning

What haven't we seen? Beleaguered people
of a dying archipelago,
where ancient women bare their ancient breasts
to bring the touch of kinship into the hearts of jackboots
marching through the creeks sowing death with machine-gun fire.
Blood on the tide, blood in the creeks,
blood on the tongues of the rivers,
blood, blood, blood, blood everywhere.
Kimse! Kimse! Kimse!

Death came through the creeks, death came upon the ancient tide,
death covered the rivers with red and black death—
children of the oil archipelago,
we saw it all. Bayoneted to scars in our souls,
we still live the nightmare of the great dying.
Now, the town crier, covered in mourning,
goes about the islands looking for you.
Kimse! Kimse! Kimse!

Who will speak for us now? The tide comes in
with empty baskets. Gas-flaring dragons assault us with acid rain.
Oloibiri is in ruins.
The rivers are dead. The sea riders have departed to slums
in the cities of the Niger Delta.
The bowls of the children are empty.
The old sigh and beat their bosoms
in remembrance of happier times.
The oil archipelago lies in great darkness while oil platforms sparkle
with diamond lights.
Kimse! Kimse! Kimse!

O lion of the oil archipelago! O spokesman of a beleaguered people!
Who will speak for us now?
Your fire is dying in the fireplace
in the middle of a rainstorm.
We shiver as cold winds come
in like mourning tides upon the homestead.
Kimse! Kimse! Kimse!

Letter to My Little Sister

I

Little sister,[5]
little sister,
I, who you have not seen
since the moments
of your first beginnings,
sit here in a cubicle
in the land of the stars and stripes,
thinking of you, thinking of you.

I know that you may not be
aware that Father is gone.
He is gone, he is gone, he is gone,
and will not return to grace
the street you have known
so well or darken the doors
of that home full of laughter
& tears & small beginnings.

I was about your age, little sister,
when this same fate struck me
like heaven's thunderbolt from the blues.
 It was indeed the blues
of suffering, of pain, of the promise
of a rudderless childhood.

My mother had left me
the same way Father has left
you. I was only a child, little
sister, what did I do to be
abandoned?

Mourning

But Mother,
she whom I had idolized
as a queen, was gone from me,
without warning of the terrible sundering,
the terrible roiling of soul, that beached me

like a whale and left me
panting hard for life's breath
on the hot coals of a deserted childhood,
a vagabond, a fugitive, from mother-care.

They had taken her away from
the village shivering,
sick, in the corridor between life
& death. But I could not tell
with my infant eyes what it was,
save that whatever it was
was terror from the womb of terror born.

I was with her as she got sicker
& sicker. I did not know what ailed her,
for I was only a child, about your age,
when the boat left with its shivering cargo
to the General Hospital in the city,
for the hospital on the island
had fallen on hard times.

A boat, a car, what does it matter
now? A car carried Father
to the General Hospital to seek reprieve;
a boat ferried Mother
away from the island to the same
hospital to seek reprieve.

My mother did not survive
the onslaught of the sniveling
beast that was attacking her.
  Father did not survive
the onslaught of the sniveling
beast that was attacking him.

The foul reaper of broken
bodies struck & my mother died
& Father died.
Denuder of homes,
foul beast with a pouch riddled
with countless holes,
someday, little sister, you will know
the miscreant when you see him.

Was Father sick?
Was Mother sick?

I know Father was sick,
but it was not necessarily
from the vagabond ailment
that stamped his forehead
with the word 'death.'

No, little sister,
Father died of a thousand agonies struck
hard into the soul-plate
of his being-in-the-world,
by a thousand lies & a thousand

betrayals, from those who deal
with long knives & short knives,
in the vast shadow of darkness,
to disembowel in broad daylight
those who come to the temples of justice,

Mourning

pleading, 'Sirs, here is the law,
do her bidding, and put your foul urges to shame.'
But not these men.
  Schooled in the arts of deception,
of villainy, of contempt for life
& anything that stands in the way
of their designs on power,
they came for Father.

The politics of transfer of power
from the military despot IBB to civilians[6]
was always going to be a tricky thing.
  The despot loved power
& knew how to wield it to corrupt
almost anyone he wanted to corrupt.
& justly earned the nickname
Maradona, not for his magical
wizardry in the beautiful game
 but for his ability to deceive and to corrupt.

When he talked of the transfer
of power from himself and the military to civilian rule,
there were many skeptics.
I was one of them, but like many
I held out hope that he would disappoint me.

The transition started
& the pols came out of the woodwork,
hungry for power
& the spoils of power.

Ah, little sister. Ah, little sister.
Trouble came with the local
government elections of 1992.
A governorship, a reelection,

in the state of innumerable rivers,
was the ultimate prize,
and to get to their lusted destination,
Machiavelli was summoned
from his grave, and made
   the chief advisor
in the unhallowed temples
 of government.

'Sir,' said they to Machiavelli,[7]
'what see you in your augury?'
'Kill, if you have to kill,
burn if you have to burn,
destroy without mercy,
if you have to destroy without mercy,
fell anything that stands in your path,
for the prize that comes with the setting sun
will be more than balm to sooth
your soul of any iniquity.'

So, the students of Machiavelli
rolled up their sleeves & went to work.
Listen, little sister, listen, if you want
to know the sad tale of Father's
death, that someday, you may pass
it on to your children, that they may
instruct themselves on how to guard
their treasured flanks when dealing
with men of this nature.

Yes, little sister, little sister.
Listen, listen. The prince
of cloaked knives and foul shadows
having spoken, his students
went abroad the land to execute

Mourning

their cloak and dagger policy—
to wit, stir up confusion, stir
up trouble, in any council
in the hands of the opposition,
and ill-invoking the laws
of the land, let the governor
declare the opposition party
council chairman, bright star of the opposition,
unfit to hold the reins of power.

Next, a caretaker
committee, handpicked by
the governor, men privy
to the plan of the scion
of Mephistopheles, woken up
from a thousand seasons in his abode
in the infernal parts of the earth.
These men, the caretaker
committee, armed with the power
from the infernal paths of the earth,
would play the role of undertaker
to trample on the law, drive it like a felon
from its hallowed chambers,
to midwife a second term
  with bottomless ballots for their master,
the governor of the state.

Thus, the land began
to rage with foul plots,
of local governments suddenly becoming ungovernable,
of the threat of caretaker committees sprouting up
like mushrooms all over the land,
& the men of Machiavelli
    marched,
& the men of Machiavelli

marched,
to the crow tunes of Mephistopheles
 until they came to the local government
 where a scion of
the Ake family held the reins.

Driven to the wall,
 his foes in front of him,
barking for his blood,
he invoked the laws of the land,
'I have a right to have
my case heard before
a competent court of the land,
to answer to the charges
you have leveled against me,
before you run me
 out of here
with your foul charges.'

'The law you talk of
was made to serve our interests,
 not yours,
not the people's,
you boneheaded fool,'
they reminded him,
laughing at him.

'You lie, you lie,'
he declared to the hounds of power.
'I know my rights,
& I will not have them
taken from me.'

'And who will enforce
those rights?' they asked

Mourning

the besieged man,
his back against the wall,
his foes in front of him,
baying for his blood.

'I know a man that will,
an incorruptible judge
that will grant me my day
in court. He will uphold the law.
He is an incorruptible judge.'

The sons of Machiavelli
rolled over in laughter.
'An incorruptible judge, a man able
to fend off our Herculean might?
 Show us the man.'

'The Honorable Justice M.D. Goodhead
 will give me my day in court.
I declare that the Honorable Justice M.D. Goodhead
 will give me my day in court.'
cried the hard-besieged man.

Listen, little sister, listen.
The men of Machiavelli knew Father,
knew his unsoiled reputation,
& cringed in terror.

'You have Goodhead,'
they said. 'We have everything else to throw
at you and at the fellow, Goodhead.
& do beware that we take no prisoners,
& strike with insane fury.'

'Very well, then,' said the besieged man,

Dokubo Melford Goodhead

'I will take my chances with Goodhead.
I dare you to do what you want to do;
but, remember, no one is above the law
& the Honorable Justice M.D. Goodhead
has brought down many a crooked man
from his high horse, making him to see
that before the law there are no lords and commoners.'

&, so, little sister, to Father's court,
the fellow came. 'Good sir, kind sir,
grant me a reprieve, that I may have
my day in court and answer to the charges that my enemies
   have hurled against me,
   before they hurl me
from the chambers where the people,
with their hard-earned vote,
       have placed me.'

Listen, little sister, listen,
& tell this to your children,
when you have them.
   Tell them
of a forbear, a proud ancestor,
who looked into the eyes
of terror, into the eyes
of naked malice, into the eyes
  of unbridled power,
into the faces of men
pledged to trample on
anything that was not bent
to serve their purpose
  & did not blink & cower in terror.

From every side,
nay from every angle,

Mourning

& from every point,
they dared Father
to grant the reprieve
to the beleaguered fellow.
'You will not stay
in that office longer
than the time it takes
for the ink to dry on
the reprieve you sign
for him,' they threatened Father.
'He will have
his day in court,'
said Father. 'The laws of the land
grant him those rights.'

'We are the law,' they told Father.

'No,' said Father
to the men from
the vast shadows
of Machiavelli's realm, 'you are not the law.
You only think you are the law,
& that is not the same as being the law.
  The laws of the land
will be upheld in my court.'

'Very well then,' said they
to Father, with unblemished hatred,
with unvarnished malice.
'We will prove to you that
we are the law
  & settle the matter
once and for all, not only
with you, but also with any
sorry fellow, who has gone

mad with these highfalutin notions
of the equality of all persons
  before the law. We hold no truths to be self-evident
  & there is none with inalienable rights;
a man makes his rights
for himself.'[8]

Listen, little sister, listen.
Commit this story to the testaments of memory.
Pass it on to your children
& let them pass it on to their children.
  Let the bravery of this ancestor
be told from generation to generation,
  for that much we owe him.

Father saw the unsheathed daggers
of the men of the shadows aimed at the nipple
of his heart and stood like a man
to take the blows that he knew must come.

To the beleaguered man,
he granted reprieve,
& the men of the shadows went abroad.
'A shady deal! A shady deal,'
they cried in the public squares.
'We smell a shady deal here.'

Ah, little sister. Ah, little sister.
As the acolytes of Machiavelli
dragged Father's name in the mud,
help came to Father from unexpected quarters.

Newswatch, the leading news magazine
in the land picked up the story
& put the lie to the smear of Father's
hard-earned reputation as an incorruptible judge.

Mourning

But the armor bearers of Machiavelli
bided their time, they bided their time,
little sister. The shield bearer of Machiavelli,
the one they called the Evil Genius,
wreaked one cunning too many
on the people by annulling the 12 June 1993[9]
presidential election, an election adjudged to be
the freest and fairest election
in the history of the country.

The country went up in flames.
The people took to the streets
& waged a battle against the despot.
Many perished in the streets of Lagos
under the fire of government troops
& armored tanks. Many disappeared
into jails from which no one
 ever heard of them again.

Yet, the people fought. We fought.
Our hardy resistance, we the people,
whom the Evil Genius had taken
to be docile surprised him &
as the reign of terror
continued on the land &
we, the people, refused to suffer
defeat, the Evil Genius saw
the hand writing on the wall
& threw in the towel.

The Evil Genius left the seat of power
in shame but left a Trojan horse,
an evil gift to the nation.
To the seat of Chief of Defense,
he appointed an infantry officer
known as the Goggled One.

Dokubo Melford Goodhead

This man, the Goggled One,
was well-versed in the sadistic arts.
He, it was, who rolled out the armored tanks
in the city of Lagos to mow down
protesters. He, it was, who flooded
the streets of Lagos with the
starched uniforms to disappear
protesters into the dark caverns
of the jails of the city of Lagos.

Ah, little sister. Ah, little sister.
The Goggled One wasted no time
in overthrowing the man appointed from the summits
of entrepreneurial success to oversee
yet another transition to civilian rule
& installed himself in power.

Lacking legitimacy, he sought quickly
to legitimize his rule by promising
yet another transition to civilian rule.
Throwing red meat to a beleaguered country
to shore up a reputation already dripping with blood,
as a hardnosed reformer,
he announced with fanfare
that he would purge the nation's
judiciary of corrupt judges,
for under the man, who appointed him as his henchman,
the judiciary had fallen on hard times.

Ah, little sister. Ah, little sister.
Father's enemies saw their chance.
The governor, whose Machiavellian campaign
Father had thwarted in the Ake campaign
was personal friends with the Goggled One,
from the time when the Goggled One

Mourning

was a midlevel officer commanding
the army base in Port Harcourt.[10]

This man's path and Father's
path had crossed before
his Machiavellian campaign. He
was head of service of the state
government at the time and his relatives,
intoxicated with the power
he held in government took
matters into their hands in a land dispute
with another family—extended relatives
of several families—confident that
the government's chief prosecutor,
the Director of Public Prosecutions,
will not press any charges against them
because of their kin in power.

They had one great misfortune:
Father was the DPP & no threat from
the secretary to the government,
which Father served, could dissuade him
from seeking justice for the family,
whose rights the SG's kith and kin
had summarily violated. Father
got justice for the aggrieved.

Ah, little sister. Ah, little sister.
Father had taken on powerful men like this man,
stepped on many powerful toes
to render justice to the poor
& the powerless. Now the daggers
leaped out from powerful cloaks.

'Away with him, away with him
to the tribunal,'[11] they cried. 'Hurry him
off to the tribunal. Hurry him
off to the tribunal.' The cries of the students of Machiavelli
rent the air. Not even the story
the leading news magazine in the country had
done on the Ake case could save Father.

Ah, little sister. No one stepped
forward to shield Father from the
deadly blows of these ruthless men.
Everyone was concerned for his own
skin and let Father alone to take
the blows of the students of Machiavelli.
   The blows fell on him
from every side, O nay, from
everywhere, from everywhere.

O little sister, O little sister,
my tears blind my eyes.
Sorrow tears my entrails apart.
My tears flow like rivers, rivers, rivers
into the vast ocean of suffering.

The hounds attacked him
with relentless ferocity.
But there he stood in the arena
of their savage wickedness,
crying, 'On the laws of the land,
I stand. On the laws of the land,
I stand. Strike, strike,
& if you will, finish the job.
On the laws of the land,
        I stand.'

Mourning

Unrelenting, they struck
their death blows. Meanwhile,
unknown to him, the vagabond
bastard of a colorectal cancer,[12]
was chewing away at his insides,
marching like an army of ants
over the archipelago of his body.

Little sister, little sister,
Father talked of pains,
of his pile returning,
and put it all to the stress
of the foul onslaught on him.

Over the phone, from here,
I said to him, 'Go to the hospital, Father.
Please, go see the doctor.
Look into the source of the pain
& the bloody stool & get a cure.'

'Son, go get a cure?'
he said to me. '& while
I am pursuing a cure,
they would fix a meeting
in faraway Abuja, and if I am not there,
what will they say?'

'The guilty is terrified of the law.
That is why he is not here.
His evil conscience disturbs him.'
'No, son, I will not give them any
fodder to feed their vicious
assassination. I will seek no cure
until the matter is settled.'

And, so, little sister, little sister,
the army of destruction ate
up his body from the inside.
& the students of Machiavelli thrust their daggers
into him from the outside.

A kangaroo tribunal
returned a verdict of insubordination to a superior.
Another kangaroo tribunal
confirmed the bastard verdict of the first one,
& suddenly Father became mortal.

'Where is the law
when I need it? Where is the law?'
he asked himself over & over again.
But his question returned to him like
vagrant echoes in an echo chamber.

Horror, horror, horror.
Misery, misery, misery.
But he did not give up
belief in the truth.

Hard, very hard, he fought
to clear his name, a name
that he had fought for with
unvarnished tenacity, a name
for which he had kept the monster
of corruption, that vile tempter,
    at bay again and again.

A name, for which he had sacrificed
every form of bribed comfort,
exercised austerity, kept himself aloof
from the circles of the land's princes,

Mourning

indeed, a name of which in the infancy
of his career, he had told us, his children,
little sister, before you were born,

'Children, I saw a man of the
law, laden with ill-gotten wealth
acquired from the sorrows
    of his fellow men
to whom he had rendered
misbegotten justice,

  & this man
haunted by the scourge
of a million furies,
now clung to life
with the help of
a million capsules
that he popped into his
body, like little children
pop candies into
 their mouths,
throughout the day.'

Ah, little sister.
Ah, little sister.
Listen. Listen.

'Children,' said he,
'I saw the fate of that man,
& I said to myself, 'Even if I were
inclined to be tempted, the fate of this man
is enough of a cautionary tale to me.
Therefore, children, your father
will not defraud any man,
will not sell justice to any man,

will not soil his conscience
with any bribe. I may die
a pauper but I will go
to my grave
in peace.'

O little sister.
O little sister.
My tears flow
like the river,
flow like the sea,
flow like the ocean.
I am helpless to stop them.
My pain flows
like the river,
flows like the sea,
flows like the ocean.
I am helpless
to stanch the wrathful tide.

A man walks
on hot beds
of coal to preserve
that which he holds
closest to the core
of his being,
& when his enemies strike,
it is what they take away.

O God, will Heaven's great
registers not record
the story of this man?
O God, will Heaven's great
registers not record
 the story of this man?

Mourning

O little sister,
O little sister,
it is not easy
for a son to see
his father fall
from the soaring
heights of immortal
deeds into the muck-ridden gutters
of mean and vengeful men.

It is like the passing away
of a nation within him.
It is like the collapse of a major
institution. O, nay, it is like
looking into the abyss
& trembling like
a tendril in the wind.

But little sister, listen, listen,
for my letter is just beginning.
Listen, little sister, listen.

To my mother's tale.
I do not know what ailed
her. Perhaps, it was severe malaria.
I do not know. I was too young to know.
But, this, I saw with my own eyes.
I saw her dying. I saw her dying
little by little every day.
& there was nothing
that I could do to save her.

The ailment ravaged her
body. The scumbag ravaged her.
Laid waste to her.

& left her
for dead on the roadside
 of pity.

On the roadside
of pity,
on the roadside
of pity,
on the roadside
of pity,
where wayfarers
turned only
to shake their heads
& spit,
for mother
was already
beyond the pale
of pity.

And what was left
of her
was only enough to fill a nameless
coffin—with no address.

She was boated home,
the same way she had been taken away,
wretched almost beyond recognition,
for the embalmer's miracle
had failed him
at the moment of direst need.
The scumbag had done
his work well.

But her proud face,
 the scumbag could not possess,

Mourning

there his withered hands
were stopped dead in their tracks.
& her proud and beautiful face
stared back at me,

when

I saw her lying in state,
well not exactly in state,
for her kind, the stateless
of the earth, do not lie in state.
They are the microminorities of the earth,
bludgeoned into contraptions
   of colonial empires
where democracy is another
word for oppression
   by the majority,
O little sister. O little sister.

Little sister, O little sister,
a din was swirling like a tornado
all around my mother,
and yet even in the midst
of the fury, I could discern whispers
among the adults, whispers
here, and whispers
there, as to whether I her little prince
could appear before his queen
in her deflowered state.

They wandered here.
& wandered there.
The whispers wandered everywhere.
The tornado swelled
unabated, scattering its entrails
all over the place.

Dokubo Melford Goodhead

& yet the whispers
continued to spread here.
& spread there,
& spread back and forth,
as Wise ones sat in council
over my fate.

Exiled from the threshold
of the mourning rain,
I waited for the verdict
of the august jury as to whether
I should step forth
to pay my last respects
to my fallen queen
or stay banished from
her presence forever.

But Mercy was my companion
that day,
added her two pieces of copper
of wise counsel
to the meeting
of the elders
and sanity prevailed
over the madness
of irrationality.

The moment came
& the steel door
of adult discretion
was thrown open
and as if by some sign
from heaven the tornado
disappeared into the folds
of a muscular silence.

Mourning

I heard the hammering
of hearts in heaving chests
& felt the sticky breath
of a communal weeping
descend like hailstones on
my six-year-old head.

But my eyes held firm
& did not water at the moment of initiation.
I saw her glorious and beautiful face
& I knew that the foul swineherd of an illness
 for all his braggart's pound,
had failed to take from her
that for which she had won
universal acclaim. I saw her.
I saw my mother. My queen. My pearl
  of inestimable value.

Fallen.
Ravaged.
Ravished.
Mute.
Blind.
Beautiful.

& yet I could not cry.
I could not cry.
The dams of sorrow
would not pay a fool's wage
to the waster, the reaper
mocking me, mocking everyone
in that sad, sad, sad corner
  of the earth.

I do not know
what it was little sister;
but I could not cry.
I could not cry.
I was no fool.
Inside me a river raged;
but I could not cry.
I could not cry.
I had no wage
to pay to the sniveling,
sneering scumbag idiot.

O little sister.
O little sister.
The death of a beloved mother
is like the sacking
of an empire
in the consciousness of a child.
He weeps. He mourns.
His sorrow is like
a razor-sharp wound.

I held my head up
as high as I could,
thrust out my chest
like the bow of a warrior,
& looked at her
whom I had loved
with all my heart.
& memories came tumbling forward
like laughing waves
riding to shore
& overwhelmed me
& comforted me,
 my bleeding-fire soul.

Mourning

'Poor child,' I heard them say,
'he doesn't understand that the
water pot is broken & he
will never be able to drink from
 it again. Even now the ferryman
 reaches the other shore.

'Poor child, he doesn't know that the
ferryman has already reached the
   other shore. & will not return
with his passenger again. Those who have
made the journey with the ferryman
  never return. Those who have
  made the journey with the ferryman
  never return. They never return.
     They never return.
Why doesn't the child spill any water
  from the water pot,
  full from the bottom
                    to the brim?'

&, so, they talked, little sister.
So, they talked little sister.
& raised a din with their chatter,
with their dirges,
with their slapping
of their ancient breasts
with palms coarsened
with decades of toil.

&, so, they underestimated the thunder
of my sorrow, O little sister.
So, they underestimated the thunder
  of my burning sorrow.

Dokubo Melford Goodhead

I know little sister
that your fate
will be no different.
Should we tell her?
Should we not?
Should we allow her
　to see him?
The once healthy house
now laid waste by
a band of forty terrors.

They will allow you to see him.
O little sister. O little sister.
　I will bet good money on that.
& little sister you will see Father
the way you have never seen him
before. A nameless terror
　　will tug at your heart.

The postman will be sure
to deliver his package: you will see Father & you will know
immediately, in spite, of the musings
of the gray and not-so-gray
hairs that Father will never
come home again.

He is now safe from his persecutors.
Those who wasted his life to oil
their engines of power can never
lay their hands on him again.

The ferryman comes. The ferryman goes.
The break of each sun brings the ferryman closer
to our individual shores. Knowing this, grasping this,
an era suddenly comes to an end for you.
O little sister. O little sister.

Mourning

Childhood scarcely begun is already
too mature to remain a child. & where
once dolls & toys
grappled with the imagination,
the harder questions of life now
break their fists
on the glass windows
   of reality.

What burden this for the shoulders
of my little sister? Scarcely out of her diapers,
already a woman? The world is not fair.
The world is terrible. These are truths,
    but there is a greater truth:
your shoulders will not bend
  your head under the foul burden.

You will not break
under the foul burden.
You will not go astray.
You will prevail. You will prevail.
    You will prevail.

Little sister, O little sister,
I do not know whether you
have been to the island
before, the island,
where Father was born,
   the island,
where my mother was born,
   the island,
where your mother was born,
   the island,
where I was born,
   & the island,

where you would have been born.
  The island
is full of stories, little sister.

She is a woman
violently taken again and again.
  She is a woman
continually turned to the sorrow of loss.

Little sister, O little sister,
have you heard any of the thousand stories
  of the island?
  No? Well, then, listen, listen, listen,
as I summon the bards
of my imagination
  to help me with the terrible tale
of tragedy, of sorrow borne again and again,
& of debilitating waste
  jackknifed into the small
    of the back.

The island heard tales
of the first war, but my tale
is not about that war,
as universal as the historians
swear it was. The island sent her
children to the second war.

Again, little sister, my tale
  is not about that war,
  even though historians
would swear on their mothers'
honor that no theatre of human
conflict
    ever rivaled it in gore.

Mourning

Not to forget
the countless souls
 that were gas-chambered
at the knifepoint
of a vagabond ideology
of racial supremacy.

No, little sister, my tale
is not about that war.
 I tell of a war
 that stole into the womb
like a cancerous tumor
the day the soldier of fortune,
Lugard, in a fit of greed,
   in a fit of megalomania,
in a fit of stealing one
 for the British empire,
rifled the pockets
 of our people,
& slapped on them a country,
  with a name
that they say that his concubine
   had drawn up
from Ali Baba's bag,
during some fanciful pillow talk.

Niger area. Niger area. Niger area.[13]

Did we not deserve a more befitting name
to inspire and challenge us to greatness?

Ah, little sister. Ah, little sister.

The nation once known as Upper Volta,
whatever that means, is now Burkina Faso.

Land of honest men. Land of honest women.
But here in the land where two rivers
meet and make their way through
the Niger Delta to the mighty Atlantic,
Niger area is still Niger area.

The name came with its compliment
  of forty thieves
  & twists & turns
worthy of a rifling enterprise
for empire, for empire.

1914.

Let
it
ring
a
violent
bell
in
your
ears,
little
sister.

1914.

That was
Lugard's
lucky number.

&, so, on Lugard's day,
at the break of a new moon,
a blind owl carrying

Mourning

the standard of justice,
flew across the confluence
of the River Niger & the River Benue,
crying, 'Robbery with violence is armed robbery.
Robbery with violence is armed robbery.'

That day an eagle,
sweeping down from the sky,
seized the body
of a stillborn child
before his parents could bury
him & tore him
to pieces before
the shocked mourners
& scattered the pieces
of the child's body
in the confluence
of the Rivers Niger & Benue.

Brother, brother, wait a minute,
you go too fast, tell me the tale
of the island & not some doleful tale
of forty thieves and an eagle
swooping out of nowhere to dismember
a stillborn child.

Pardon me, little sister,
if my metaphors grate
on your ears of innocence,
a man in deep sorrow,
you must allow, should be
permitted some sympathy,
   & the empathy
 of uncensored ears. Permit me,
then, to continue my tale.

Dokubo Melford Goodhead

For even as I tell my tale,
I know that those ears
full of the leprous tale
of father's passing
are no longer innocent.
Owls' droppings have
found their home there,
  &, even now, the terrible tale
    lies at the threshold of a splintered vessel.

Hear me, then, little sister,
    O little sister,
for my tale is long, & I must make haste,
    lest haste
overtake me, and my tale
    is left half-told.

&, so, in the year
of Lugard's lucky
    numbers, 1914,
an eagle swooping out of nowhere
seized a stillborn child
 & tore him to pieces
in front of shocked mourners.
The pieces of the body
   of the child,
the eagle scattered
   in the confluence of the Rivers Niger & Benue
   and in the creeks & rivers of the oil archipelago
of the Niger Delta.

The island, little sister,
    is one of many pearls
tucked into the bosoms
    of the mangrove forests

Mourning

of the Niger Delta.
The forests of pain.
The forests of sorrow.

The forests of dark spirits.
The forests of a thousand goblins.
The forests of a thousand hallucinations.

The ancients saw the gore
& grime of the scattered flesh
of the stillborn child in the rivers of the oil archipelago
& knew straightaway that a searing knife
had been thrust in the back of the oil archipelago.

A conference of gray hairs
gathered in every village square.
The town criers cried. The children
     wept.
The ancients bared their ancient heads.

Grannies threatened to expose
their ancient breasts in village arenas
  but Lugard was steadfast, believing
that he had got his lucky numbers.

'I know a good hand,
when I see one,'
 he said. '1914 it is.
& 1914 it will be.'
&, so, 1914 it came to be.

Brother, where are you going?
Sister, where are you going?
The wayfarer asked everyone
he met on his way.

Dokubo Melford Goodhead

My tale is a tale
of unending sorrow.
Pray, show me the way
that I should go.

But no one listened to the wayfarer,
for the highway and the destitute portions
of the earth were his only home.
The highway and the destitute portions
of the earth were his only refuge.

Soon, little sister, O little sister,
Lugard's lucky numbers
spawned more lucky numbers.
Colonialism, O colonialism,
where the Enlightenment, where the cosmopolitanism,
  where the Golden rule?
The Delta's neighbors
with whom they had intermarried, with whom
  they had supped
in common bowls, with whom
they had danced joyfully
    in countless arenas,
showed their lucky numbers,
championed their lucky numbers,
& the peoples of the Niger Delta
raised a din of protest.[14]

But luckless numbers
  get you nowhere
    in the arena
of Lugard's lucky numbers.

The lucky numbers triumphed in the parliament of numbers.
The lucky numbers triumphed in the school of numbers.

Mourning

The lucky numbers triumphed in the market of numbers.
The lucky numbers triumphed in the real estate of numbers.
The lucky numbers triumphed in the commerce of numbers.
The lucky numbers triumphed everywhere.

Soon their neighbors filled
with the wonders of what lucky numbers
can do foisted a hegemony of lucky numbers
like a triumphant flag over the luckless numbers
 of their minority neighbors.

Beware, little sister,
of luckless numbers.
They carry nothing
but the entrails of misery.

But Lugard's lucky numbers
were running out, politicians in flowing robes
spread their wide garments
over the till of the land, and numbers
disappeared, and numbers
appeared in Swiss banks
& other secret places.

Paradise is here, they swore.
Why wait for another paradise,
when we can create one here
for our children & generations
    of theirs?

& many a man by the name
of politician aspired to carve
out his own little paradise,
an eternal estate, for himself
& his seed, here on earth.

Dokubo Melford Goodhead

Paradises. Paradises. Paradises.
In a wilderness of want.
In a wilderness of suffering.
In a wilderness of despair.

Little sister, O little sister,
nimbus clouds began to gather
  upon the land.
Vultures began to circle
  the land.
A crouching fear found a prey
  in the hearts of men.

& while those
that had lucky numbers
dreamt sweet dreams,
& those that had luckless numbers
dreamt fallow dreams,
Lugard's boys struck in
the midst of a misbegotten night.

Across the land in the North,
the scion of a royal family
fell in a hail of bullets.
His lieutenant was damned
with the same numbers,
and the great war of numbers began.[15]

Brother, where are you going?
Sister, where are you going?
asked the wayfarer of everyone
he met on his way.
My tale is a tale
of unending sorrow.
Pray, show me the way
that I should go?

Mourning

But no one paid heed
to the hapless wayfarer.

Beware, little sister, of myths.
There are good myths.
There are bad myths.
Humanity cannot survive without myths.

Let me simplify it, little sister,
O little sister: no man can survive without a myth,
for when a man wakes up with a cheerful face in the morning,
believing that the day will go well for him;
he believes a myth, for right on his doorstep
may be lying in wait the clutches of tragedy.

Even if he were to believe
in a day laden with sorrows,
it is still a myth, for on that day
may come to port the cargo
of all he has worked for in his life.

&, so, little sister, myths
are good. Myths are wonderful.
But, when, myths are used
to cause sorrow to others,
they become highway robbers
lying in wait at the elbow
of every fork in the road.

Chemical Alis
in the hands
of a Saddam Hussein.
Tonton Macoutes
in the hands
of a Papa Doc Duvalier.

Dokubo Melford Goodhead

Paul Okuntimos,
Hamza Mustaphas,
& David Omenkas
in the hands of a Sani Abacha.

And, so, little sister,
O little sister,
the war of numbers
started. In Lugard's vast
country of numbers,
three numbers
stand out as aces.

Our neighbors
held one.
In the West of the country
stood the people
with the second ace.
And in the North
in flowing robes
& overwhelming numbers,
stood the people
with the third ace.
Ace no. 3
marched across
the Rivers Niger and Benue
to join ace no. 2.
The pact of Ares was established
between the two.
& the two aces
threw their hats
in the ring against one.

Caught in the crossfire
of the war of the three aces

Mourning

were the people
of the island and their brother islands
in that vast archipelago
of pain and suffering
buried in the Niger Delta.
Numbers. Numbers. Numbers.
Poured into the oil archipelago.
Poured into the Niger Delta.

& numbers upon numbers
had their numbers permanently retired.
The bloody butcher of a bastard war
ran up its lucky run of numbers,
nearly two million and counting,
& the blood of a stillborn
child continued to bleed
    its luckless numbers
into the laps of the oil archipelago,
into the laps of the Niger Delta.

There was death in the air.
There was death on the land.
There was death in the rivers.
There was death everywhere.
Everywhere you turned, you saw
the face of death, the cries of the dying,
& the last gasps of men, women, & children
leaving the threshold of life
with the eternal boatman.

Listen, little sister, listen.
I watched my mother die
a slow death. There was no doctor on the island.
Mother had been known
for a strong constitution before

the war. The war robbed her
of her strong constitution, gave
her a body prone to illness.
Yes, little sister, in that war of luckless
  & lucky numbers,
my mother was one of the luckless
      ones.

Listen, little sister, listen.
When I was a little child,
the island used to perform
a yearly ritual of mourning
& celebration. A dirge here.
& a dirge there. A reminiscence
of their unlucky run of luckless numbers,
of children cut down in their cradle,
of men & women cut down in their prime,
of ancients cut down in the dusk
of their nightfall.

Listen, little sister, listen.
The numbers of the departing
summoned a parliament of vultures
from every corner of the earth.
A parliament of ravens
from every corner of the earth.
Come & eat & drink to your fill;
their messengers sent word to the
four corners of the earth. & the
parliament of vultures lasted a thousand seasons.
                             & the
parliament of ravens lasted a thousand seasons.
Mother was invited to that feast,
but heaven spared her flesh
from the talons of the loathsome brood.

Mourning

Machine-gunned down in the laps
of the creeks,
a child heaved in her womb,
while with the messenger
of the night she fought
the battle of her life.

The harbinger of death took
both of her feet from under her.
Her lifeblood flowed into the
creeks of the Niger Delta.
But her number was not called that day
at the gathering of that foul brood
that spread like a sweeping swarm
of locusts all over the land.

The moment of dying gone,
it would come another day.
A feckless health would be her
luckless number thereafter.
The sound of war would beat in her ears.
Its incubi would haunt her sleep.

The foul reaper would sound his raven horn.
Faraway in the secret places
of the earth, the rivers would heave
& heave again. & a lone boatman
would begin his silent journey
across worlds. The paddle dips
into the river, yet the river does
not make a sound. The birds of passage
beat their wings violently against
the wind, yet there is no trace of them.
The night rings with curious voices,
yet its sounds are not heard even

by the fellow about to embark
on the journey to that other shore.

The ferryman comes.
The ferryman comes.
But no one sees the moment
of his coming.
The war came
& with it the harbinger
of death. & mother
fell on the side of Lugard's luckless numbers.

Brother, where are you going?
Sister, where are you going?
asked the wayfarer of everyone
   he met on his way.

My tale is a tale
   of unending sorrow,
cried the wayfarer.
   Pray, show me the way
that I should go to shake
off the cries of the dead;
but no one listened to the wayfarer
   & his passing
fell like a pebble
without a trace
into the sea of life.

Little sister, O little sister, listen.
I don't know how many times
I have cracked the nuts of sorrow
or how many times I have
wandered to the edge of the abyss.

Mourning

My sorrow is great. My pain is maddening.
My terror is greater than I can bear.
I see terror before me & terror after me,
& terror standing on my left side,
& terror standing on my right side.
I flee, but cannot flee. I run
but it is into a sea of madness.

& ocean of tormenting pain
    engulfs me.
  A beggar clutches me
hard by the throat. The poor man
  demands from me
the last penny of my sanity.

Hold on brother, I say,
  my lot is worse
than yours, but the beggar
    grabs me
  by both my hands.

I struggle to be free,
but I am unable to free
  myself from
  the steel grip of the beggar.
Now, the trace of the beggar
    is upon me.

The trace of his wretched loneliness
is seared onto my forehead &
  all that see me flee,
  for I am a vagabond stricken
  with the terror of the travails
  of the oil archipelago,
& madness engulfs me on all sides.

Dokubo Melford Goodhead

I was born on a day of sorrow
   into a house of sorrow
& my days have been filled
with the bleakness of sorrow.
Even before I was ready, sorrow
seared off my foreskin
with its broken knife,
& circumcised me on the shards
of a violent harmattan morning.

I was left crying & bleeding
& the world heard my lachrymal
   burst of pain
& shut their ears,
for the cry of my pain
was too vicious
even for circumcised ears.

When the day of my naming came,
I was named for my father's father,
& the old women called me Papa,
   even though I was nothing
but a whelp in an unconscionable
world.

But fate would begrudge me
even this little honor & sought to castrate me
with the jagged edges
of a tree stump.

I fell bleeding into a sea
of smiling feces
and my nostrils filled
with the terrible stench of suffering
have wept ever since
the tale of my botched castration.

Mourning

When morning crawls
through my door,
it announces itself with weeping & gnashing of teeth.
When the sun shines upon me,
it beats upon me with unrelenting savagery.
When the rain falls,
it threatens to sweep me away
in a flood of bruising tide.
I stand but cannot stand.
I kneel but cannot kneel.
I am knocked senseless
into the shit of searing pain.
& when I raise my head,
I am hammered under into the underbelly
of a well-fed despair.

Little sister, O little sister.
Darkness fills the threshold.
& the threshold creeps upon
the house with a crouching terror.

Against the wall the back
of the orphan is pressed.
Nowhere to go, nowhere to turn.
& the hangman comes upon him
with a determined face.

I pray to my Maker. I count out
my last hours on the beads of sorrow.
Each bead tells its tale. Each bead
weeps out the moment of its passing.

I was born on an island.
The name of the island
   is suffering.

Dokubo Melford Goodhead

I was born on an island,
whose river once beat with the lives
  of a million million creatures.
Now, the name of its river
is dead & gone, dead & gone,
  all dead & gone.

I was born on an island.
Once, its creeks
creaked with the crush of crabs
& periwinkles.
Now, the name of its creeks
is crushed to death, crushed to death,
all crushed to death.

I was born on an island.
    Once its wells
overflowed with the water of life.
Now, the name of its wells
is filled with the blackness of death,
filled with the blackness of death,
all filled with the blackness of death.

I was born on an island.
Once its skies were festooned
with the gaiety of the wonders of a thousand dancing clouds.
Now, the name of its skies
is blackness and sorrow,
blackness and sorrow,
all blackness and sorrow.

Little sister, O little sister,
  my beloved island
is now an island of sorrow.
Blood flows into its river,
flows into the sea, flows into the ocean.

Mourning

Red blood.
Black blood.
Black blood.
Red blood.

Innocents are cut down day and night
& yet the island is fed with more blood.
& yet the river is fed with more blood.
& yet the sea is fed with more blood.
& yet the ocean is fed with more blood.
& when the blood pours it pours.
& the river is never the same again.
& the sea is never the same again.
& the ocean is never the same again.
& the fish depart & do not return,
for laughter is gone, where once
laughter was plentiful like the sea
at high tide mating with the
bamboo roots of the mangrove forest.

The fish depart & do not return,
for sorrow has scarred their hearts,
& loathsome death has felled their kindred.
The fish depart & do not return,
for the island is filled with unbearable shame.
The unbearable shame of naked terror,
the vice-like grip of terrible pillage,
the terrible pillage of gas flares, oil spills,
the oil spills that destroy river & land & people,
the people reaching out with beggar bowls
   to indigenous colonial masters,
indigenous colonial masters full of ethnocentric bullshit
   and murder in their eyes.
Murder. Murder. Murder.
In the bloody oil archipelago.

Dokubo Melford Goodhead

Rapine. Waste. Misery. Ah, little sister,
I hear the despairing hollowness of needless murder,
the despairing hollowness of needless suffering,
of man's great inhumanity to his fellow men.
I hear. I hear. I hear. I hear the
crushing heaviness of irreplaceable loss.

The fish depart & do not return,
for the island is like a woman whose thighs
have been forcefully thrown apart
by a band of marauders at a busy crossroad
& all that pass by lower their pants
& have their fill of her, or shamelessly relieve
the fury of their foul burden on her prone body.

The fish depart & do not return,
for all that is left of my beloved island
is the stench of unbearable suffering,
and a signpost inscribed with a prayer to God:
O Great One, if my children come
this way again, do not let them
return as microminorities in a land put together
by a soldier of fortune for the thieving chests of a colonial empire.
My children have borne the yoke
of suffering, of misery, of rape, of death.
Have mercy on them, O Great One.
Have mercy on them, for their suffering
is arduous and long and their reprieve
is like the bite of an adder
left to fester until the night falls
over tortured eyes, pleading, pleading, pleading
for the right to live.

What Year?

O Mother
What year was it now
that you died?
1971 or 1972?
I am sorry, O island woman,
if I took a moment
to remember
the year of your death.
I am still your son, O Mother,
the boy you bathed in the morning
cold to send off to school.

Confused

O Mother,
do you remember,
that I was never able
to bring myself to leave you and Grandma,
tear myself away
from the homestead, where island birds sang all day,
until the last of the
school bell was going off
as if a hurricane
was coming from
the sea to the island,
like a masquerade with a million heads, holding a whip
in his hand, a whip as long
as the oil archipelago,
as long as these desecrated
islands of misery, of sorrow, of death.
You have crossed the great sea
now—and I, what do
I do with myself?
O sweet Mother, woman
of the oil archipelago?

You Died

I remember the day
they took you
to the city.

They were
taking you to the General Hospital
because the hospital
on the island
was a scarecrow.

I remember the day
they took you to the city
because the hospital on the island
was a mockery of the art of Hippocrates.

I remember it as if it was
just yesterday, O Mother.

The white garment prophet
talked of witches and wizards
until he ran out of sacrifices
to tell Grandma to offer to
wicked, water spirits.

O Mother, what could I do?
I was only six.[16]

They took you to the hospital in the city,
O Mother, after the white garment
prophet had already killed you
with his lies.

The Fallen City

I did not see
you again, O Mother,
until the day they brought you back
in a makeshift coffin.

I still remember
the weeping of the old women,
of palms rising
to strike aged bosoms,
the piercing wail, the dirge,
as if a city had fallen
and was lying in ruin.

Forgive Me, Mother

Forgive me, Mother
that I could not weep,
when I saw your body.
O Mother,
I could not shed a tear.
O Mother,
I could not even slap
my bosom
with my palms
like the old women
were doing beside
your body.
I could not weep,
O Mother.
I could not weep,
for I was too mad
to weep.
O Mother, forgive me.

Looking for the Hiding Place of Death

The swordfish cut me
through the heart with its sword
and I howled and howled and howled,
running here, running there,
looking to see whether I could find death
and fight him to the finish
& bring you back to the homestead,
O Mother; but I could not find death
on the day I was ready to die.
& neither the island birds
nor the island winds could take me
to the hiding place of death.

I Never Saw the Fisher of Sorrows

I never saw the fisher of sorrows,
could not even catch his scent in the wayward
sea breezes from the great sea,
and none could tell me where to find him,
until the day they were
putting you in the earth.
O island woman. O woman of the oil archipelago.
I looked at the gaping hole in the earth,
looked at the coffin
and wanted to jump in and stretch out my being
on the gilded wood;
but, suddenly, I remembered the song
you used to sing to me,
as you gave me my bath
to get me ready for school &
O Mother, O island woman,
I discovered what I must do.

The Road Before Me

I saw the road before me, O Mother.
I saw the road before me, & I have been on that road ever since
The road led me to death,
to the hailstorm, to the blizzard,
to the hurting rain.
I saw the end several times.

O island woman. O woman of the oil archipelago.
I saw it like I saw it on your face
the day they took you from the island
to the General Hospital in the city.

But each time I looked into the eyes
of the fisher of sorrows,
I heard your voice, O island woman, O woman of the oil archipelago
telling me the road that I must take.

No Longer a Boy

I wanted, I wanted, I wanted to go with you
in the boat
that took you away
from the island, for a son should
not leave his mother's side,
when his father
is away from the
homestead; but Grandma
would not let me.

How I cried & cried & cried
to see you go,
O island woman,
O woman of the oil archipelago.

But Grandma said
that a man does not cry in the face of adversity.
Grandma said that
Father was away to make a better tomorrow
for his wife & children.[17]
& his absence asks me to be a man.
  Six. O Mother. Six.
& I was no longer a boy
  but a man.

In Memoriam – for Mother

Epilogue I

A terrible pain fills my heart, a searing pain. Pain, pain, that
will not go away. I see the boy out in the open sea.
The terrors crash about his raft. Hell, wind, & fire. They crash
upon his head. Lightning. Thunder. Thunderbolts.
Sky and earth are one in one blind & raging amalgam.
But his raft is still bobbing up & down in the teeth
of the raging sea. I see him go down. I see him rise.
I turn away but the pain is still there.
Raging. Raging. Raging. &, suddenly, I hear your voice calling,
　calling, calling,
'Son, roll your raft out to sea. Roll. Stay the course.
Roll. Roll. Roll.' I turn to look in the teeth
　of the raging storm, but you were gone.

Epilogue II

Baptism of fire! Baptism of rage! Raft breakers let loose like a
sea full of wayward sharks. Where sky, where sea?
I cannot tell. Ah, what rage of fire and light is this? What inferno?
What rage? What rage? Then, suddenly, the sky clears
& there is calm.
& once more, I hear school bells ringing,
in the windward archipelago
where seagulls go to rest
& the singing of the weaverbird never stops.
Early morning sun bursting to bloom like a rose,
woman of elegant beauty,
mother, mentor, guardian. I see you now. I see you clearly.
I see you
as if it were only yesterday. I see you laughing. I see you smiling.
& I smile too. & I laugh too. I smile. I laugh. I smile.
It was like the old times all over again,

Mourning

O woman of the windward archipelago.
O woman of the tiny island in the laughing archipelago.
Then, suddenly, you were gone.

Epilogue III

'Hurrah,' she says. 'Hurrah! The boy is now a man.
Roll out the drums.
Call sea and land; let the talking drum call everyone
to the feast of songs & dance in the town square.
Oh, let the drums descend from ancient rafters,
where sea smoke lingers over the fireplace.
Tell the tales of warriors.
Let the little island
& the archipelago come alive!'

O mother, breaker of myths and paths,
watch me, then, dance the sea-smoke dance
of warriors returned from the terrors of the high seas
laden with the bounteous harvest of the sea.
O Mother, watch me dance.

Lithe feet of laughter, lithe feet of soul, she is the first to dance.
O mother, is this you? Is this really you?

Suddenly, I awake and realize
that it is only a dream, & she is gone.

The Man Who Came from Death to Life

I have come from death to life,
O Mother.
A million seasons
I have spent out in the rain,
out in the blizzard, out in the tempest.
It was chilly out there.
O Mother.
I was cold and sick,
sick to my bones,
sick to the soles of my feet,
sick like
a beached whale
on alien beach.
I thought I would die
but I remembered you,
O island woman. O woman of the oil archipelago.
& I lived.

Notes

1.   Household diesel generator. It is widely used throughout Nigeria by those who can afford them.

2.   This is a poem about the oil-related militia insurrection in the Niger Delta in the 2000s. I kept getting news from home, of daily bloodbaths and massacres in the once peaceful islands of Nigeria's oil archipelago, where years of oil exploitation and pollution had destroyed the rivers and caused the massive flight of islanders to the slums of the cities of the Niger Delta.

3.   On the night of October 20, 2020, Nigerian troops invaded a great gathering of peaceful protesters at the Lekki tollgate and opened fire on them, leaving several people dead. The protesters were protesting police brutality.

4.   Maxwell Oditta was a classmate in the Department of English at the University of Nigeria. He and I became close friends. At about the time I was mourning his death, the newly elected government of General Buhari was trying to reel in one of the most respected militia leaders during the militia insurrection in the Niger Delta. Government Oweizide Ekpemupolo aka Tompolo was regarded by many in the Niger Delta as a true revolutionary in the mode of Isaac Adaka Boro, a former Student Union leader, who led an insurrection against the Nigerian government to call attention to the plight of the ethnic minorities of the oil

Notes

archipelago of the Niger Delta. Boro declared the Niger Delta Republic on February 23, 1966, and held out against the Nigerian military with a few dozen youth like himself for twelve days.

Tompolo was spearheading the fight for the establishment of a Niger Delta Maritime University in Okerenkoko, his home town, after he and other militia leaders reached a peace agreement with the government of President Umaru Yar'Adua, in order to give a maritime-based university education to the tens of thousands of island youth who had no future. Whereas President Yar'Adua greenlighted the project, the government of President Buhari decided to move against both the university and its champion.

Tompolo went into hiding. After an initial contingent of Nigerian troops wreaked havoc in Okerenkoko in the search for him, the Nigerian government decided not to escalate matters. Tompolo lived to see the government of Buhari reverse itself and build the university, which is now called Nigeria Maritime University. This poem was written at about the time Tompolo went into hiding, with the threat of a new round of violence against the islanders of the oil archipelago of the Niger Delta from the government of Nigeria hanging in the air.

5.   My little sister, Lolia, was about six years old when our father died from colon cancer. I was about her age when my mother died at the age of twenty-eight on the island of Buguma, in the Niger Delta, of an ailment that I still don't know.

6.   General Ibrahim Badamosi Babangida, popularly known as IBB, overthrew a fellow military General, Major-General Muhammadu Buhari, in 1985, and seized power. General Buhari, himself, had staged a coup to overthrow

the civilian government of President Shehu Usman Aliyu Shagari in 1983. IBB elevated corruption to the status of state craft, but he earned his nickname Maradona after the legendary football player Maradona, for using cunning and trickery as arts of power.

7. During IBB's rule, it was often said that the thinker that most influenced him in the art of governance was Machiavelli. The politicians quickly learned from him how to play politics like students of Machiavelli.

8. Nigeria had adopted the British system of government from her former colonial master, Britain. In the second Republic, the country decided to adopt the American system of government but made the system unworkable and unstable by concentrating power in the center and giving control of the oil wealth of the Niger Delta to whomever controlled the center. The ideas that might makes right and the end justifies the means are the grundnorm of Nigerian politics.

9. Chief Moshood Kashimawo Olawale Abiola, an enormously wealthy businessman and philanthropist, popularly known as M.K.O. Abiola, won the election. But staying true to his nickname as a trickster always up to some trickery or cunning, IBB cancelled the election. Widespread revolt followed that forced him from power. On his way out of office, he quickly set up an interim government and appointed the business technocrat, Chief Ernest Adegunle Oladeinde Shonekan, to head the government. IBB's defense minister, General Sani Abacha, who had rolled out tanks to slaughter protesters on Ikorodu Road, a major road in Lagos, drove Chief Shonekan from office less than three months

after he was installed in office and instituted one of the most brutal military governments in the history of Africa.

10.   One of those elite was the governor of the state, on the platform of the National Republican Convention, during the Third Republic (NRC). To secure a second term, the governor decided to use NRC councilors to foment trouble in the local government councils under the opposition party in the state, the Social Democratic Party (SDP), and use that as a pretext to dissolve the councils and replace them with caretaker committees, made up of his fellow party men and women, who would then use their positions on the council to deliver the vote to him during the governorship election.

To carry out this plan, the governor needed a pliant judiciary, from the chief judge of the state to the state judges in the various local government areas (LGAs). The plan took off in the Andoni LGA, where the chairman decided to challenge the governor's dissolution of the LGA council and his removal as chairman in the court. In effect, he asked the court to prevent the governor from dissolving the council until the governor has proven in court that he has valid reasons to do so. The governor had not expected any judge in the state to have the guts to give such reliefs to the SDP LGA chairman. It was the second time that my father was ruling against the governor for abuse of power. The first time was in a land dispute involving his extended family and another family when he was Secretary to the Government of Rivers State.

These rulings and similar rulings against other very powerful persons in the state made my father very powerful enemies. They decided to take him down through General Abacha's Judicial "Reform" Tribunal.

Notes

11. Though my father's persecutors could not prove that my father issued the restraining order on the governor preventing him from removing the SDP Andoni LGA chairman without first showing cause for removing the chairman from office because he took a bribe from the chairman, the Abacha Judiciary Tribunal still recommended that my father be retired for defying the advice of the chief judge of Rivers State that he not issue the preliminary injunction against the erstwhile governor.

12. While my father was appearing before the Abacha Judiciary Tribunal to clear his name, he came down with colon cancer, unknown to him at the time. Even after he started passing blood in his stool, he refused my advice to check into a hospital for fear that his accusers would accuse him of using illness as an excuse to dodge the tribunal. The work of the tribunal dragged on and on and while that was happening, the cancer was spreading from his colon to the rest of his internal organs. When the cancer forced a shutdown of his kidneys, he finally checked himself into a hospital, where he was given the news that he had terminal cancer.

13. The country got its name from Flora Louise Shaw, the wife of Frederick Lugard, the man who, on the invitation of British merchants who had been trading with the various coastal states in what is now the Niger Delta region, came to that corner of the world and began a colonizing conquest that ultimately became Nigeria. The wars that led to the making of Nigeria started when the British merchants decided to conquer the coastal states and dislodge them as middlemen in order to have direct access to the goods and lands in the interior. The coastal states had been trading with the Europeans since the Portuguese first got there in

the 15th century. They put up a stiff resistance to British conquest. King Jaja of Opobo's defiance of British rule over the city state of Opobo, following the Berlin Conference of 1884-1885, where Europe partitioned Africa amongst the European powers, led to his capture and exile in Barbados. In 1895, King Koko of the Nembe kingdom led a raid on British merchants at Akassa. The kings of the coastal states were unwilling to cede their trade to the British merchants or come under British rule. They seem to have had prescient knowledge of what would happen to their descendants in the wake of British colonial rule.

Today, the once proud coastal states are now shadows of their former selves. Nigeria's oil wealth is drawn mostly from the rivers surrounding their islands, rivers that have suffered such oil pollution that they are now dead rivers. The Niger Delta is today known as the oil pollution capital of the world. The worst and the most oil-related human rights abuses and state-orchestrated violence have taken place in the Niger Delta. Several Nigerian governments have frequently crushed both peaceful and violent protests with Nigerian-military-led bloodbaths. In November 1999, following the killing of seven Nigerian policemen by an armed group of young men in the coastal town of Odi, the Nigerian government, instead of using its security intelligence to fish out the young men, sent the Nigerian army to raze the entire town to the ground. Anyone who was not able to flee the onslaught was slaughtered. In the midst of enormous oil and gas wealth, the coastal people of the Niger Delta remain some of the poorest people in the world.

14. Imperial Britain divided colonial Nigeria into three regions, along the lines of the three major ethnic groups

in the country, the Hausa-Fulani in the Northern Region, the Yoruba in the Western Region, and the Igbo in the Eastern Region. Into these regions, imperial Britain forced the over three hundred and fifty other ethnic groups. These minority ethnic groups immediately came under double colonialization, the colonialism of imperial Britain and the colonialism of the major ethnic group of their region. Imperial Britain did this to bring down the cost of colonial rule and maximize colonial profit for itself. The cost in human suffering since then has been staggering.

15.   On January 15, Major Kaduna Nzeogwu, son of a Fulani woman and an Igbo father, who was born and raised in the northern city of Kaduna, led a group of young officers to overthrow the government of Prime Minister Abubakar Tafawa Balewa. The young officers had grown tired of the widespread allegations of corruption and the instability in the country as a result of ethnic conflict, as the three major ethnic groups—the Hausa-Fulani, the Yoruba, and the Igbo—fought political battles with each other in order to take charge of the center. The coup plotters had planned to kill the top politicians in the three regions, except, some say, Chief Obafemi Awolowo, the former Premier of the Western Region. A difference in philosophy with his former deputy, Chief Ladoke Akintola, on how to position the Action Group, the party he formed, nationally led to a breakup of the party.

Chief Akintola took his breakaway faction, the Nigerian National Democratic Party, into a political alliance with the ruling Northern People's Congress of Prime Minister Balewa and control of the Western Region, developments which led to widespread instability in the Western Region. Chief Awolowo was accused of treason, a charge many

Notes

regarded as trumped up to get him out of the way of Chief Akintola, and imprisoned. The coup plotters, it was said, saw him as the most capable politician to lead the country and had plans to free him from prison and put him in charge of the country.

The plan failed for two key reasons. Major Emmanuel Ifeajuna, an Igbo officer, who was in charge of killing the top two Igbo politicians, Nigeria's titular president, Dr. Nnamdi Azikiwe, and the Premier of the Eastern Region, Dr. Michael Okpara, failed to carry out his assignment. Meanwhile, the officers in charge of the coup in the Northern Region and the Western Region killed their targets, including the most powerful politician in the land, Alhaji Ahmadu Bello, leader of the NPC and Premier of the Northern Region. In the Western Region, where Major Victor Banjo, a Yoruba, and Major Timothy Onwuatuegwu, an Igbo, led the coup, the coup plotters killed Chief Akintola and the most senior ranking Yoruba officer in the Nigerian army, Brigadier-General Samuel Adesujo Ademulegun, but failed in their mission to kill the most senior ranking officer in the Nigerian military, Major- General Aguiyi-Ironsi, an Igbo. Upon his escape from the coup plotters, Major-General Aguiyi-Ironsi rallied troops and crushed the coup, after which he installed himself as head of state. In May 1966, General Aguiyi-Ironsi issued Decree 34, which abolished Nigeria's federal form of government and put in its place a unitary form of government.

The Northern Region reacted by carrying out a counter coup in July of that year to pull the Northern Region out of the country. The young Northern military officers successfully carried out the coup, killing General Aguiyi-Ironsi and massacring many Igbo officers, but before they could carry out their project of taking the Northern Region out of the country, the British High Commissioner had a marathon meeting with them to persuade them not to pull the Northern Region out of the country as the new country would miss out of the riches from the oil and gas in the Niger Delta, which were at the time mostly in the hands of Shell British Petroleum. The young officers listened to him and kept power for themselves, appointing Colonel Yakubu Gowon as head of state. Displaying bad faith, Colonel Gowon kept the infamous Decree 34 for which the North had carried out the counter coup. After Northern politicians whipped up anti-Igbo sentiments in the North that led to the mass slaughter of the Igbo in the North, Colonel Ojukwu, an Igbo, who was in charge of the Eastern Region asked for the replacement of the unitary form of government with an even more radical federal form of government, a confederal government, so that each region could organize its affairs as it pleased without intervention from the central government. Colonel Gowon and the Hausa-Fulani elite refused to give up their newly acquired power to run the country as a unitary state. Colonel Ojukwu pointed out their hypocrisy and the genocide against the Igbo in the North and refused to settle for anything less than a confederal Nigeria.

With the country hurtling toward civil war, General Joseph Ankrah of Ghana tried to broker peace between the two sides at Aburi, Ghana. Colonel Ojukwu thought that he got Colonel Gowon to agree to a confederal form of government at Aburi but when Colonel Gowon insisted on keeping the unitary form of government in place on his return to Nigeria, Colonel Ojukwu decided to take the Eastern Region out of Nigeria to form a new country, Biafra.

Notes

Civil war erupted. With the backing of Nigeria's former colonial master, Britain, who, from colonial times, trusted the elite of the feudal North more than their counterparts in the South, to protect Shell BP and other British economic interests in Nigeria, the Nigerian government imposed an ironclad economic blockade on Biafra. By some estimates, almost two million Igbo and ethnic minorities of the former Eastern Region, most of them children, died from starvation due to the economic blockade.

16. My older sister says that our mother died in January of 1972. I have always thought that she died after my 6th birthday, April 8 of that year.

17. My father was getting his law degree at the University of Lagos, in the then capital of Nigeria, when my mother died.

Acknowledgments

I want to thank Brett Hill, managing editor of the Cornerstone Press, editorial assistants Cale Jacoby and Adam E. King, and the rest of the editorial team for their invaluable work with me on the book. I also want to thank Amanda Leibham, production director of the press, and her production team for the beautiful cover design for the book. My thanks also go to Dr. Ross Tangedal, director of the press, for the excellent work he did with the galley copy, his invaluable suggestions, and for putting everything together. It was such a joy to work with every one of them.

DOKUBO MELFORD GOODHEAD is a Nigerian poet, scholar, and researcher. He received his Ph.D. in English and MFA in creative writing from the University of Washington, and is a former professor of interdisciplinary studies at Spelman College. He lives in Atlanta, Georgia.